Sign Language Workbook for Kids

Learning Made Simple

Speedy Publishing LLC
40 E. Main St. #1156
Newark, DE 19711
www.speedypublishing.com

Aa

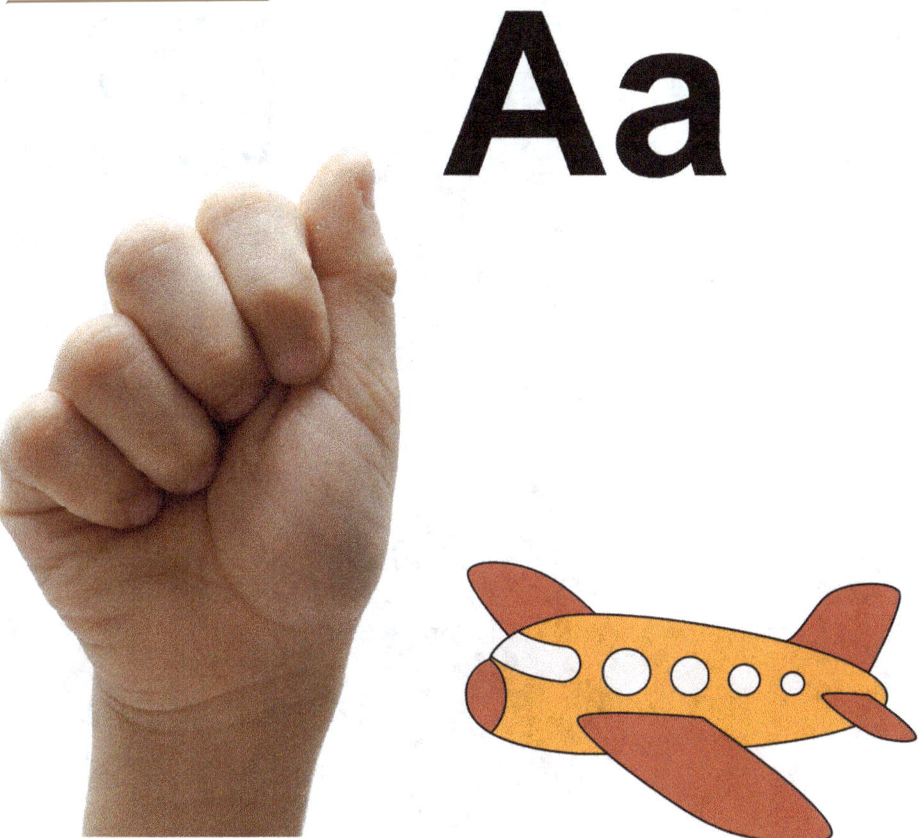

A is for

airplane

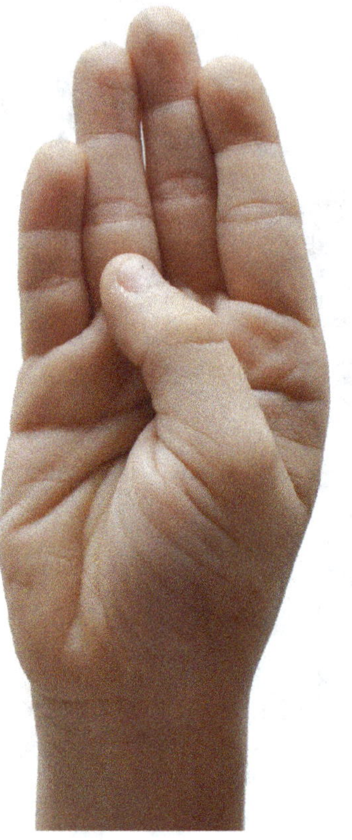

Bb

B is for
bells

Cc

C is for

cup

Dd

D is for
dog

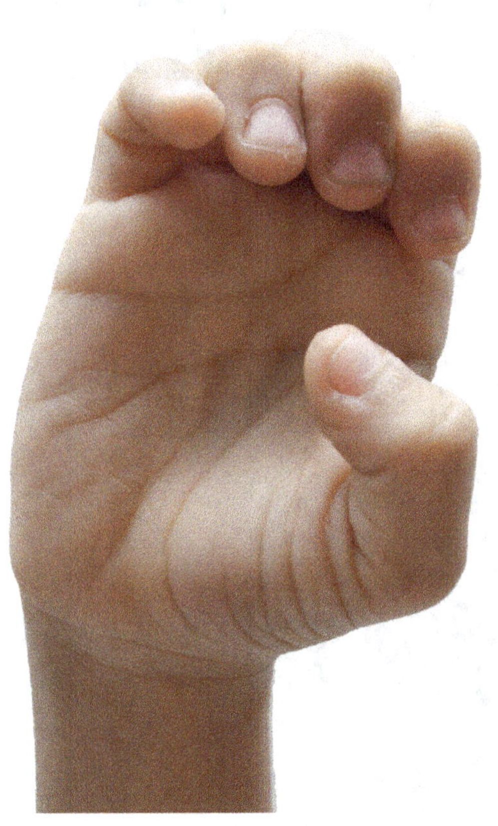

Ee

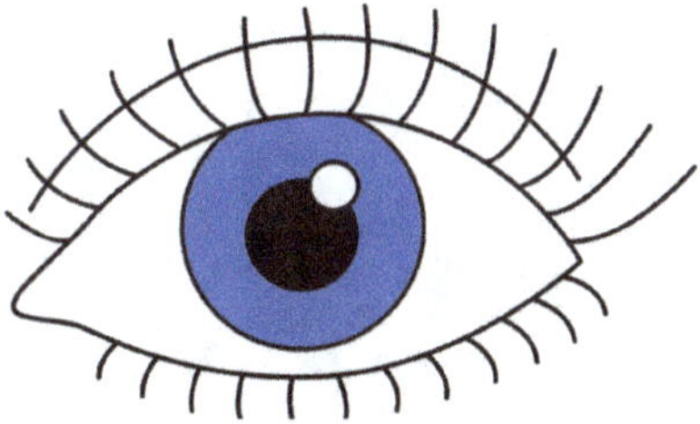

E is for

eye

Ff

F is for fire

Gg
G is for
grapes

Hh

H is for

house

Ii

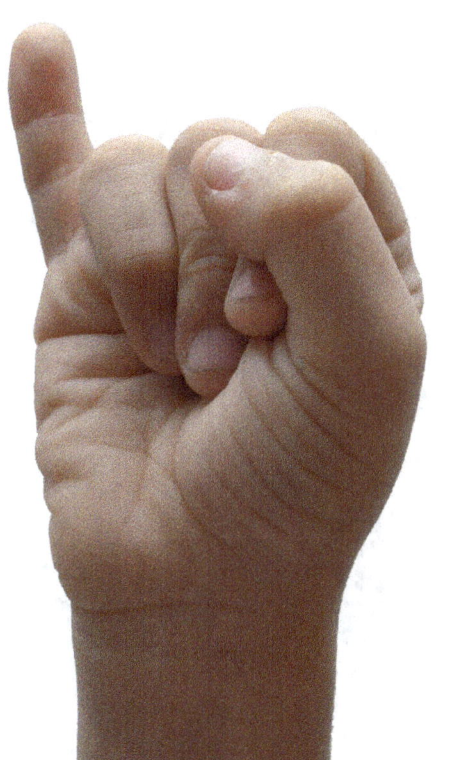

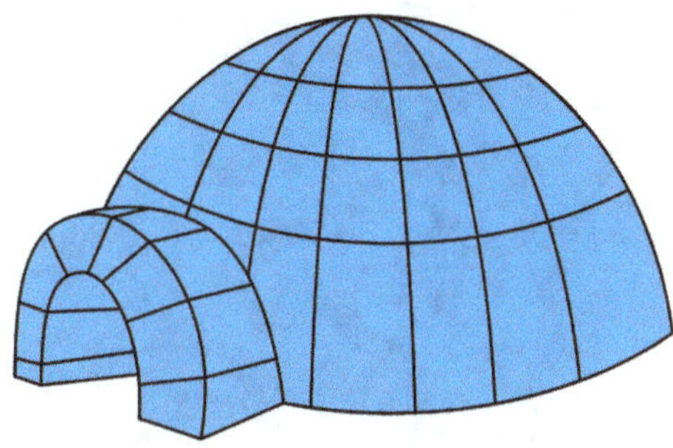

I is for

igloo

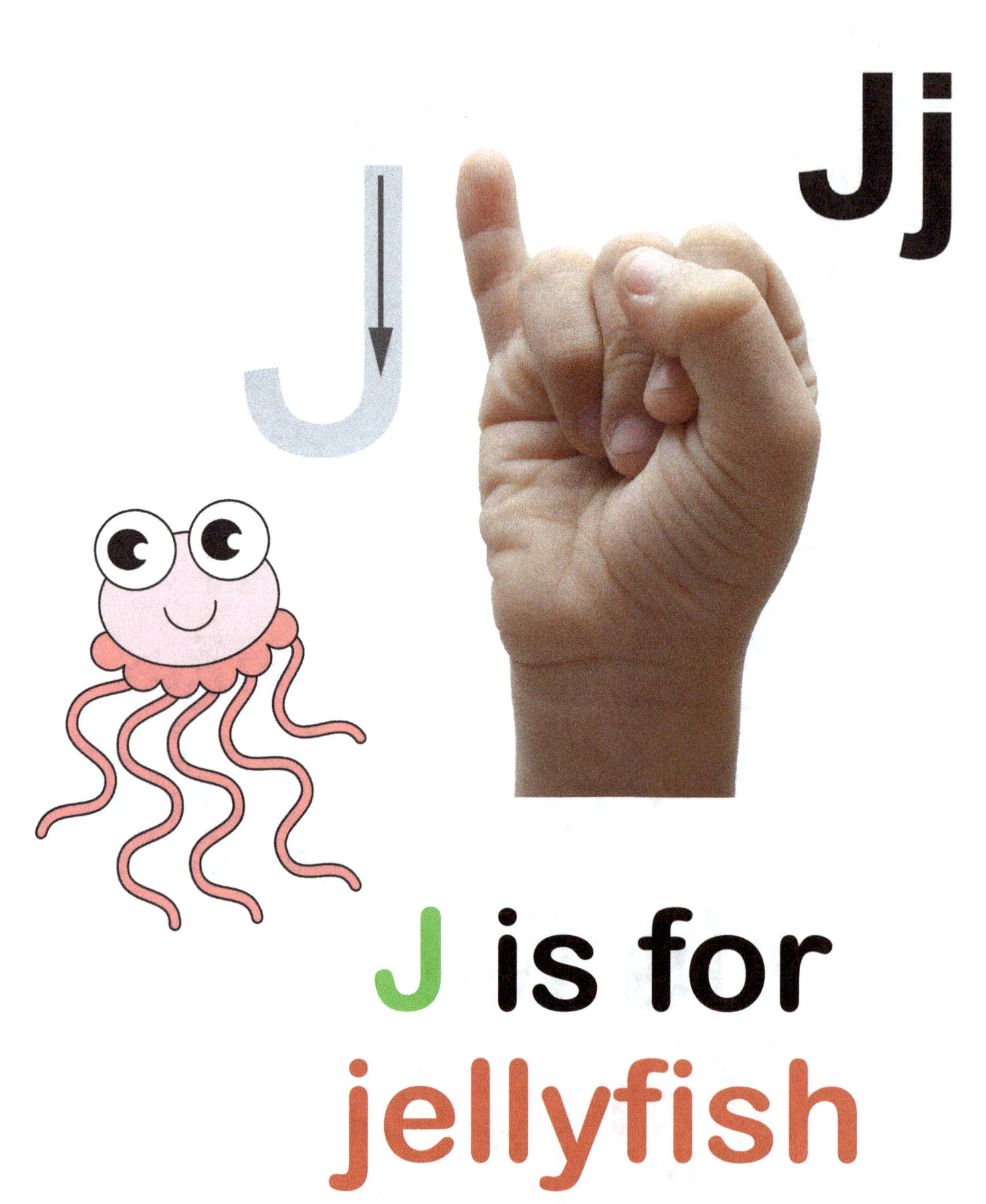

Jj
J
J is for
jellyfish

Kk

K is for
kite

Ll

L is for
leaf

Mm

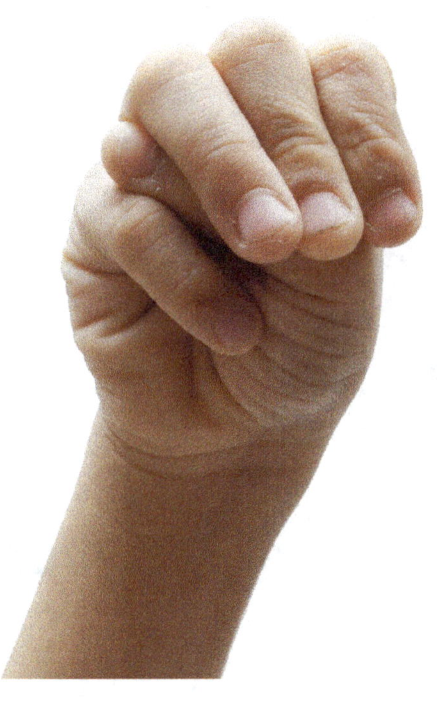

M is for
monkey

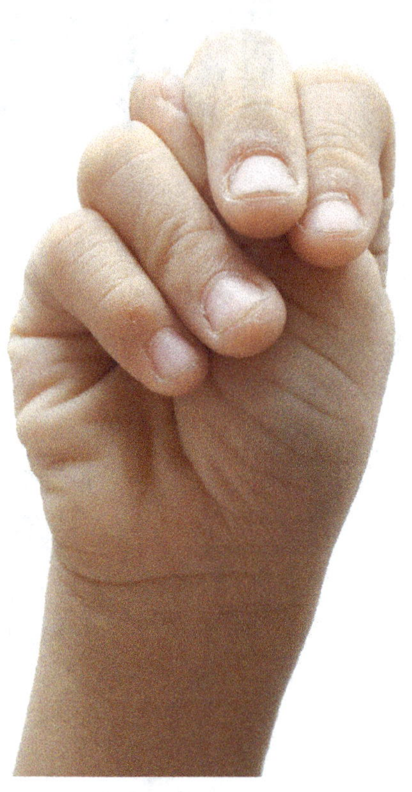

Nn

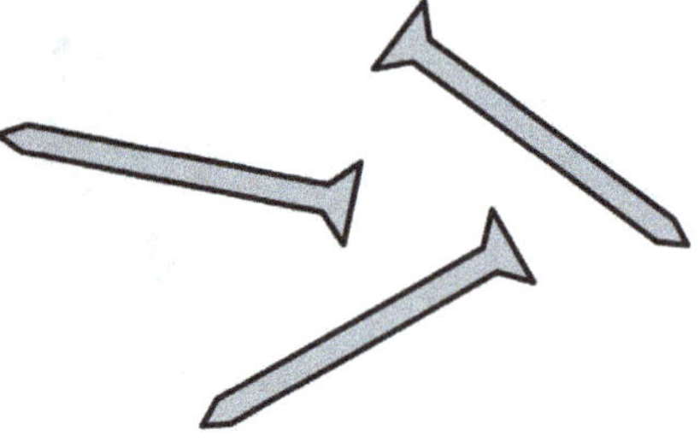

N is for
nails

Oo

O is for

orange

Pp
P is for
pear

Qq

Q is for

question mark

Rr

R is for

rainbow

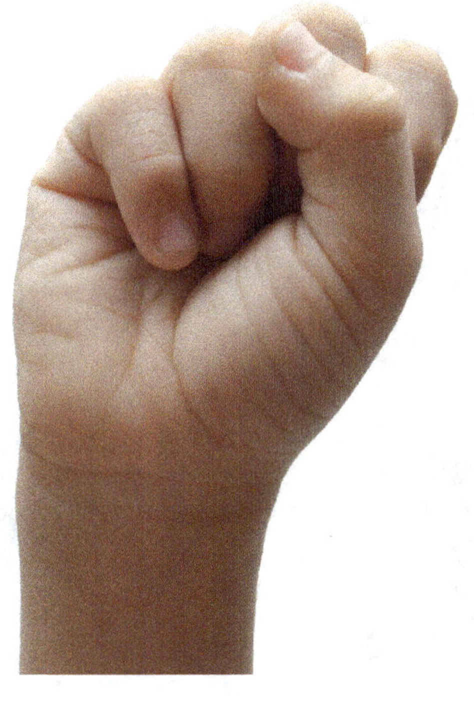

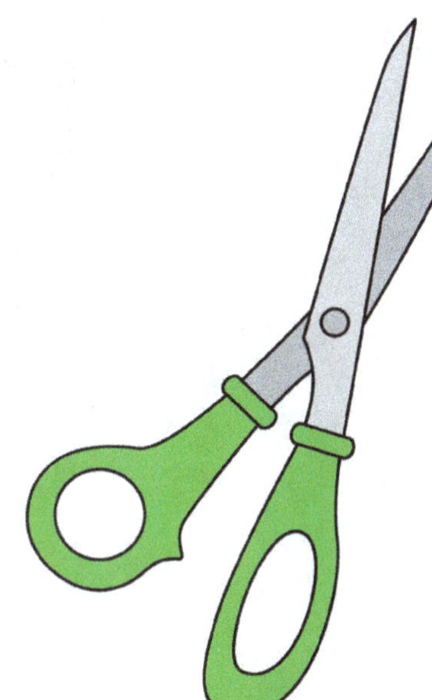

S is for

scissors

Tt

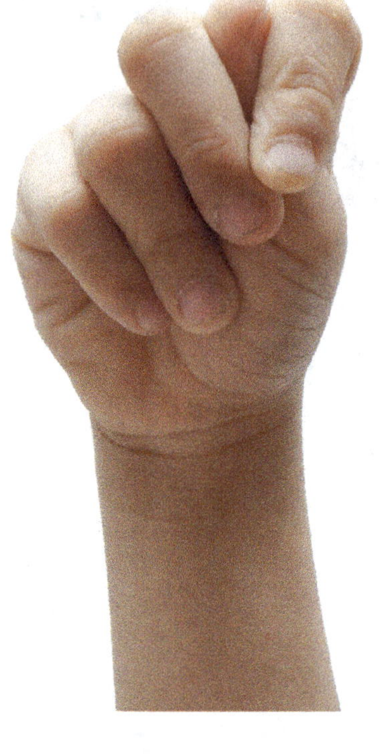

T is for
tree

Uu

U is for
umbrella

Vv

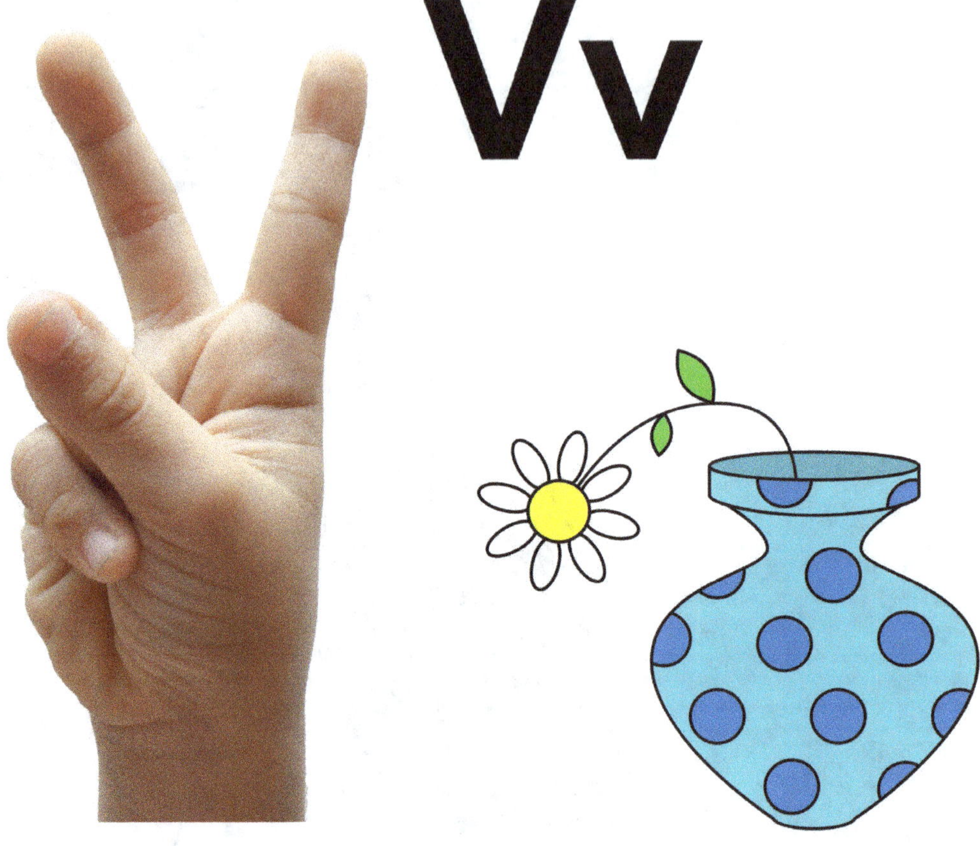

V **is for**

vase

Ww

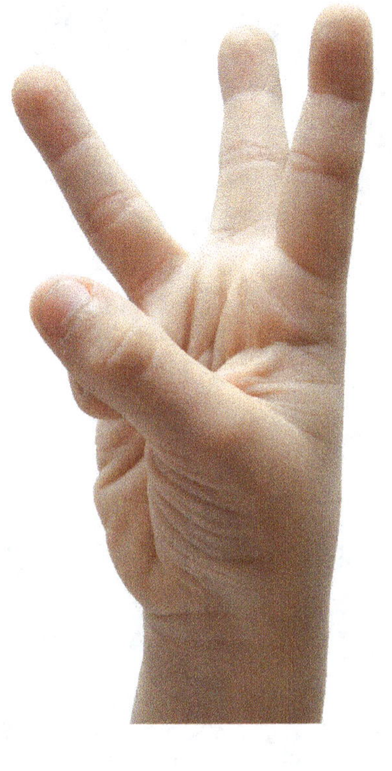

w is for
watermelon

Xx

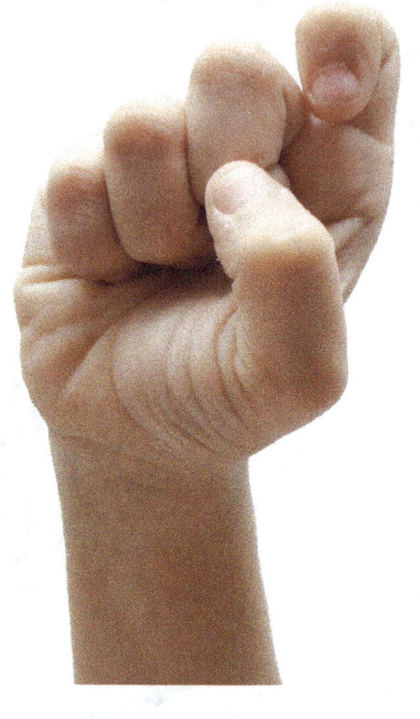

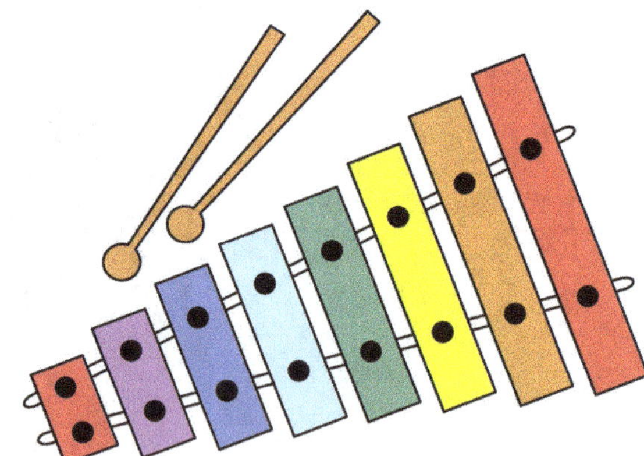

X is for

xylophone

Yy

Y is for

yarn

Zz

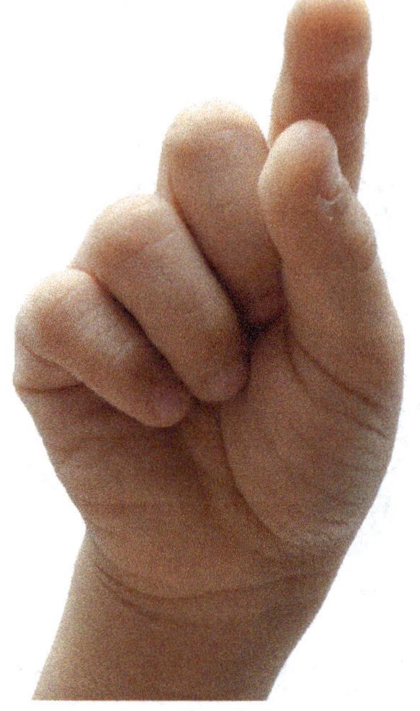

Z is for
zebra

Exercise #1: Color the hand signal for letter A

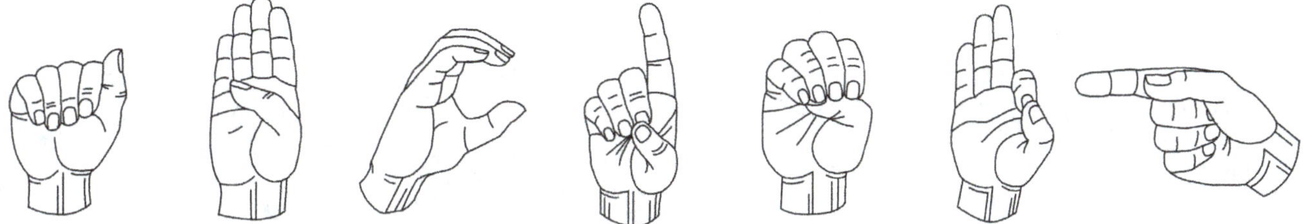

Exercise #2: Color the hand signal for letter C

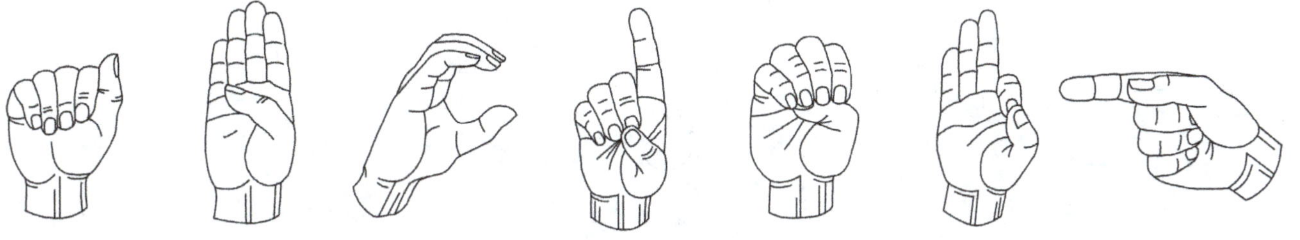

Exercise #3: Color the hand signal for letter E

Exercise #4: Color the hand signal for letter H

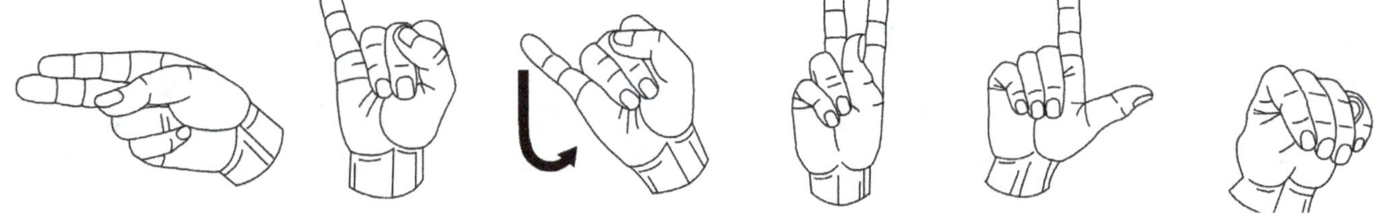

Exercise #5: Color the hand signal for letter J

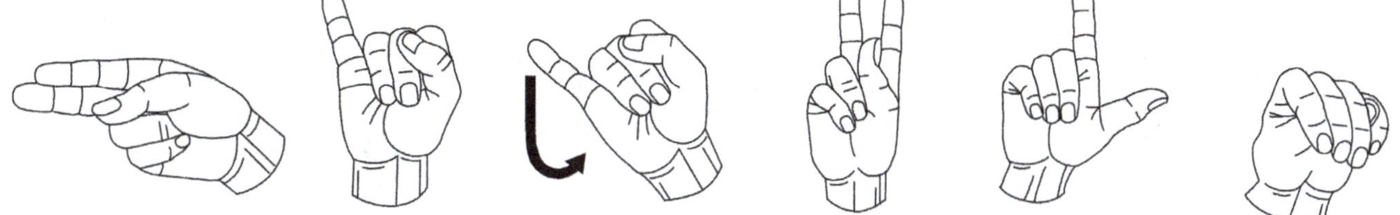

Exercise #6: Color the hand signal for letter L

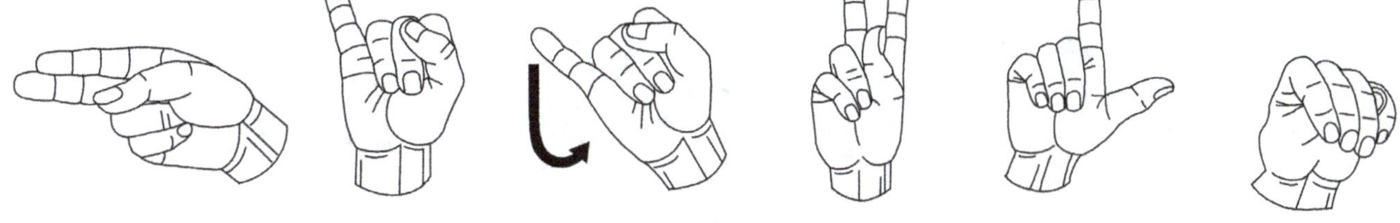

Exercise #7: Color the hand signal for letter N

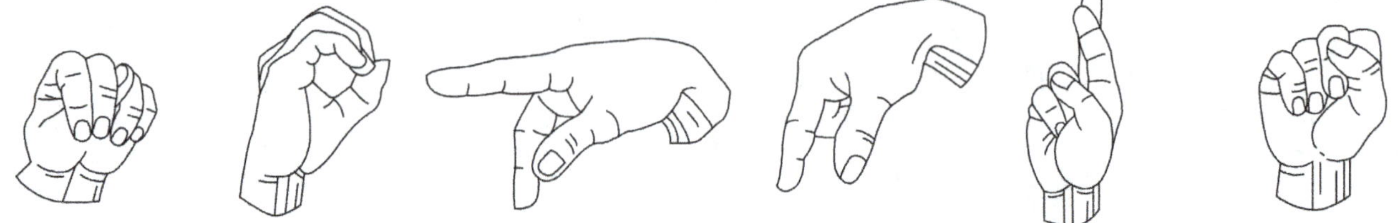

Exercise #8: Color the hand signal for letter P

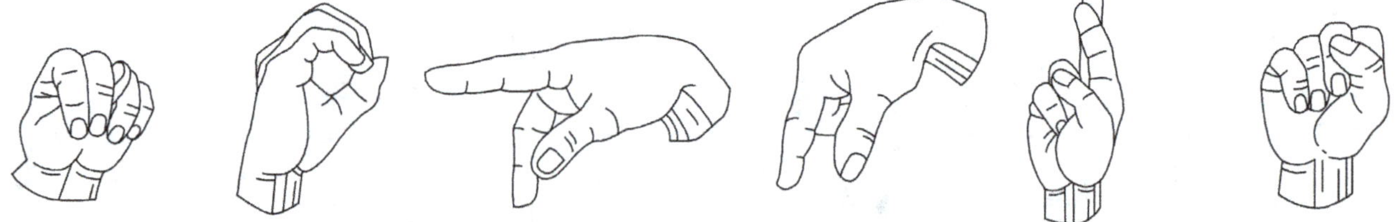

Exercise #9: Color the hand signal for letter R

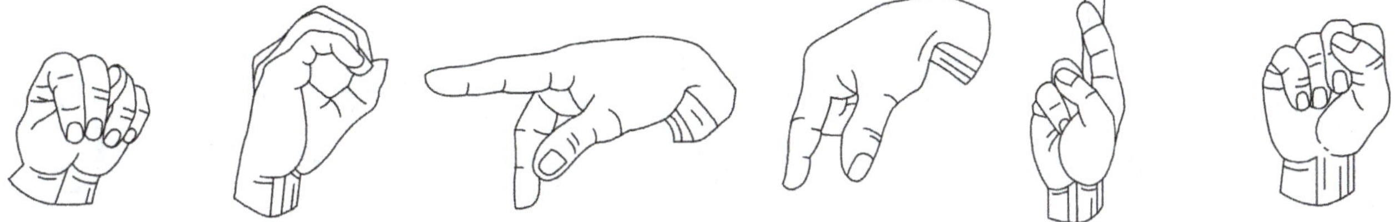

Exercise #10: Color the hand signal for letter T

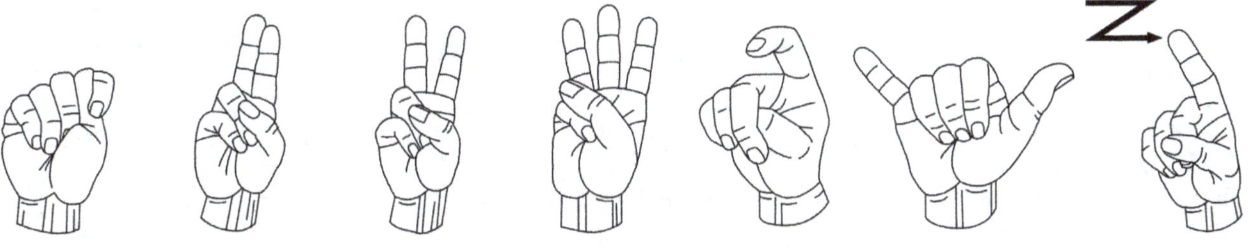

Exercise #11: Color the hand signal for letter V

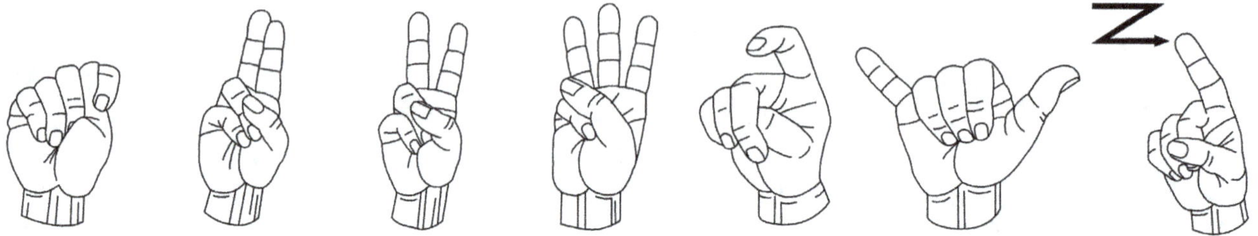

Exercise #12: Color the hand signal for letter X

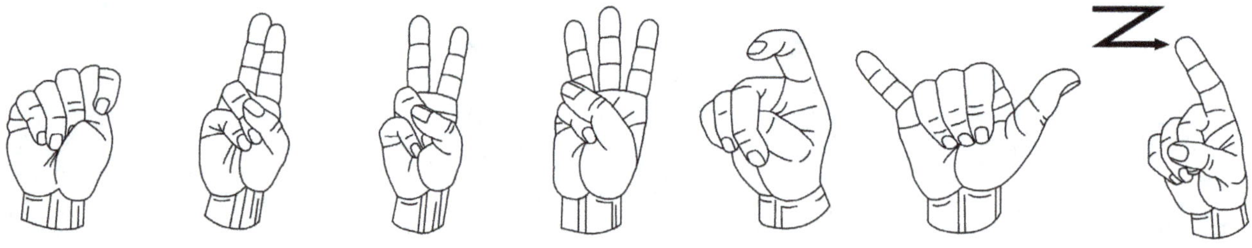

Exercise #13: Color the hand signal for letter Z

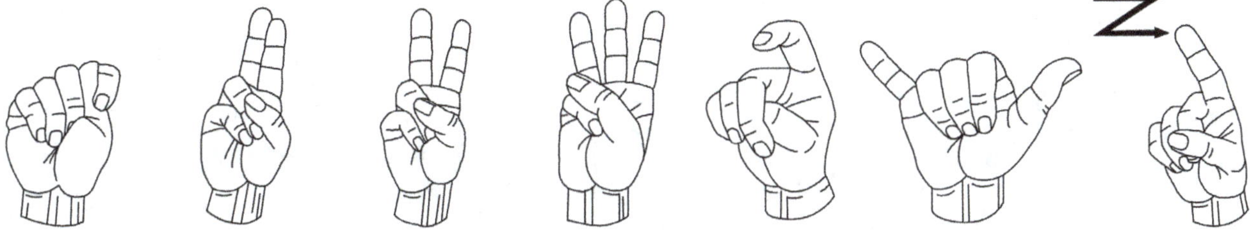

Exercise #14: Color the hand signal for letter B

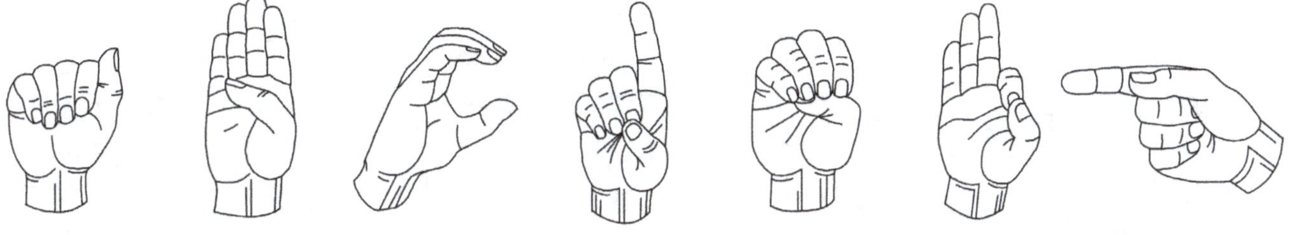

Exercise #15: Color the hand signal for letter D

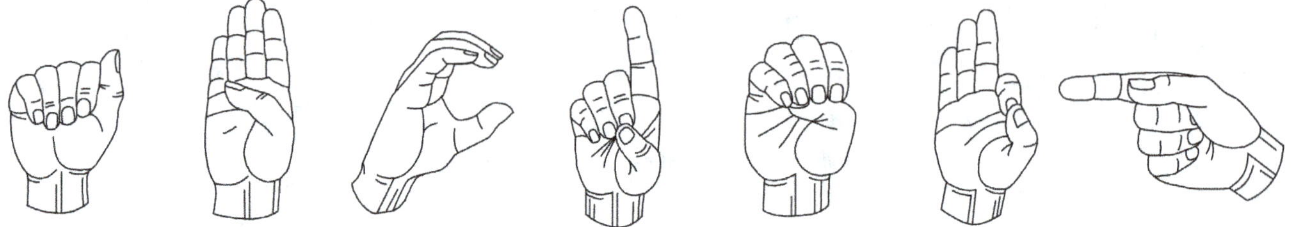

Exercise #16: Color the hand signal for letter F

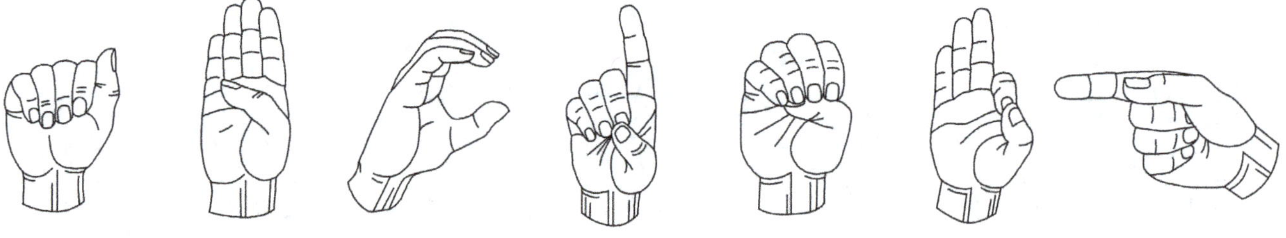

Exercise #17: Color the hand signal for letter G

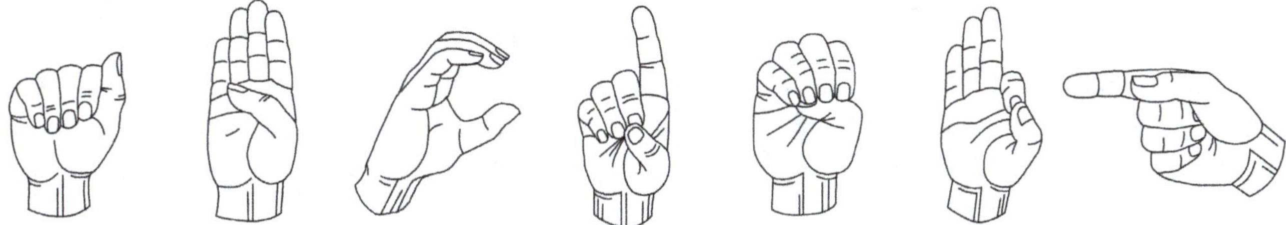

Exercise #18: Color the hand signal for letter I

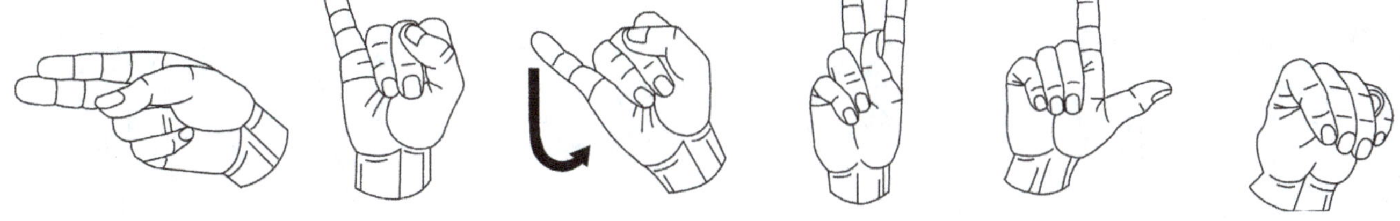

Exercise #19: Color the hand signal for letter K

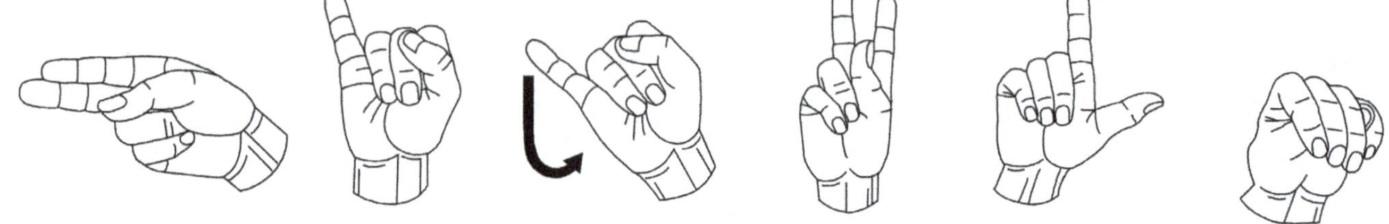

Exercise #20: Color the hand signal for letter N

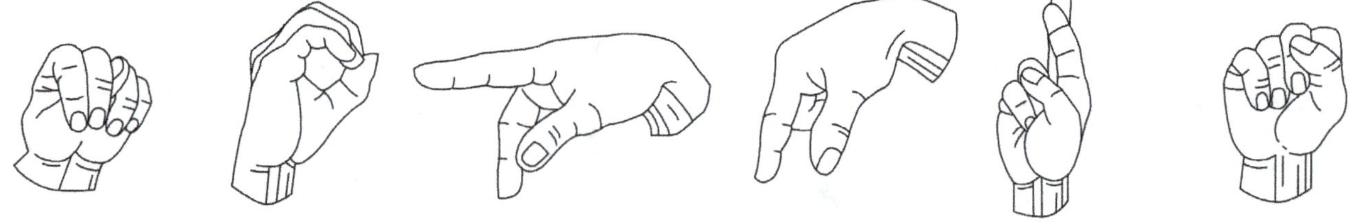

ANSWERS

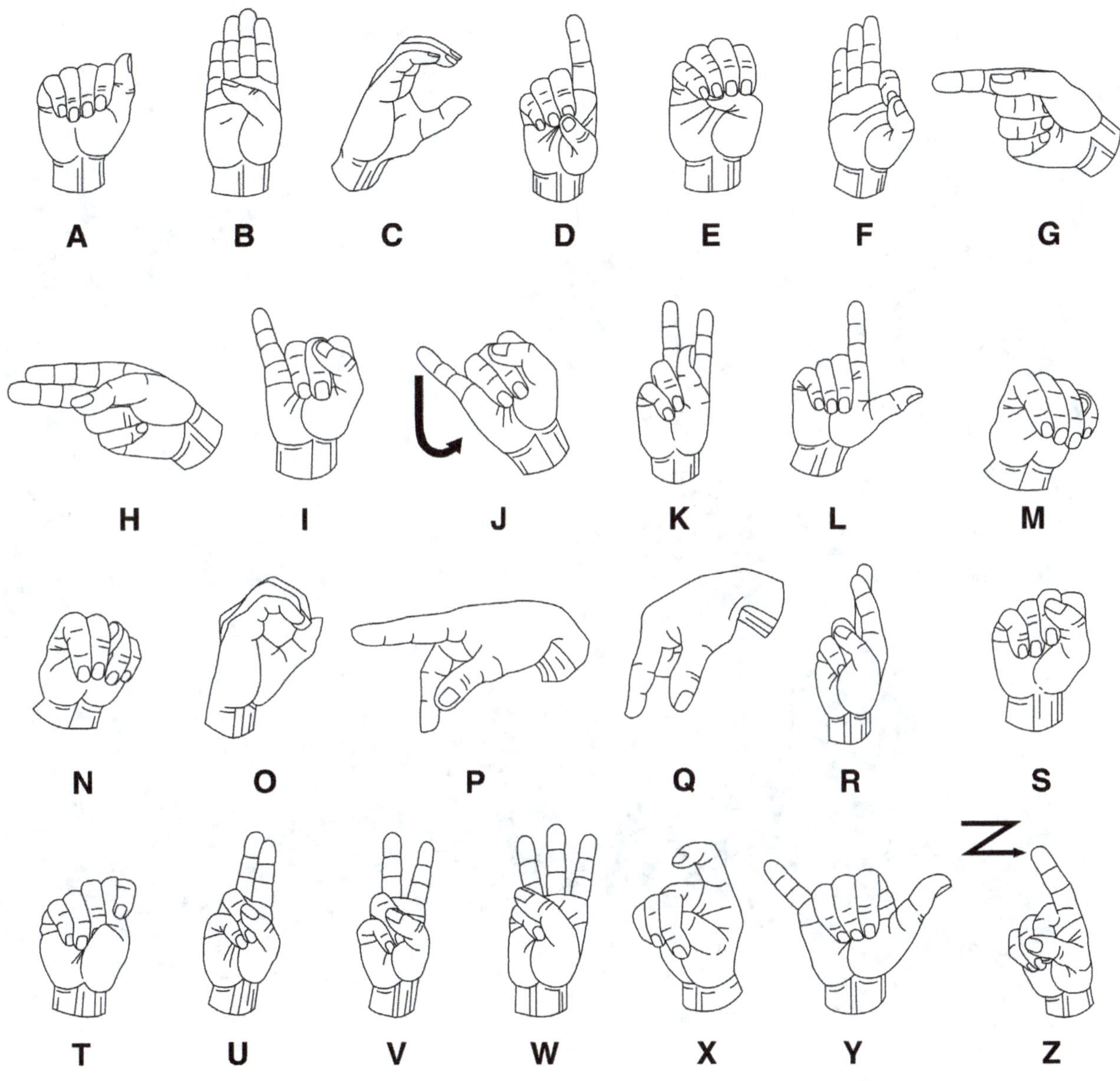

Visit
BABY PROFESSOR
EDUCATION KIDS
www.BabyProfessorBooks.com
to download Free Baby Professor eBooks
and view our catalog of new and exciting
Children's Books